DK ESSENTIAL MANAGERS

Interviewing People

DEEDEE DOKE

London, New York, Munich,
Melbourne, and Delhi

Editor Daniel Mills
US Editor Margaret Parrish
Senior Art Editor Helen Spencer
Production Editor Ben Marcus
Production Controller Hema Gohil
Executive Managing Editor Adèle Hayward
Managing Art Editor Kat Mead
Art Director Peter Luff
Publisher Stephanie Jackson

DK DELHI
Editor Saloni Talwar
Designer Ivy Roy
Design Manager Arunesh Talapatra
DTP Designers Pushpak Tyagi, Preetam Singh

First American Edition, 2009

Published in the United States by DK Publishing
375 Hudson Street, New York, New York 10014

09 10 11 12 10 9 8 7 6 5 4 3 2 1

ND141—November 2009

Published in Great Britain by Dorling Kindersley Limited

A catalog record for this book is available from
the Library of Congress.

ISBN 978-0-7566-5554-9

DK books are available at special discounts
when purchased in bulk for sales promotions,
premiums, fund-raising, or educational use.
For details, contact: DK Publishing Special Markets,
375 Hudson Street, New York, New York 10014
or SpecialSales@dk.com.

Color reproduction by Colorscan, Singapore
Printed in China by WKT

Discover more at
www.dk.com

Contents

4 Introduction

CHAPTER 1

Planning the interview

Introduction

The key to success for any organization is its people. Getting the right people depends on how an organization recruits, and a fundamental element of the recruitment process is interviewing.

As the business environment becomes more dynamic, organizations' needs change, and so do the skills they require of their employees. Moreover, simply having the right skills does not guarantee that a candidate will benefit your organization. Today's most creative and progressive recruiters recognize that understanding the aptitudes, attitudes, and motivations of their employees is essential to ensuring that the people they hire represent the best possible fit for current vacancies. As a result, those who conduct job interviews on behalf of their organizations not only hold the present, but also the future of their employer squarely in their hands. That is a big responsibility.

The goal of *Interviewing People* is to guide you through the minefield of interviewing candidates: organizing interviews and other supplementary activities, helping you to ask the right questions, deciding which information sources you should consider in finding out who the person really is, and preparing the groundwork for successful partnerships between the new employees and your organization. The end result should be to make interviews rewarding for candidates and recruiters.

Chapter 1

Planning the interview

Interviewing a potential recruit is a long and complex process, but the reward is seeing the person you interviewed contributing to your organization's success and happy in their job. Achieving that success takes careful planning.

Developing a checklist

Your checklist is your step-by-step guide to ensuring that you and your organization make the most of the candidate interviews. Create it at the very beginning of your recruitment process so that you can always visualize where you are at a given moment and what you need to do next.

TIP

PLAN TILL THE END

Include time in your plan to check references and make an offer once you have chosen a candidate.

Planning to plan

Preparing for and conducting an interview involves a number of steps. However, the actual interview is only one part of the process. Your checklist should cover the steps required before the interview, during the interview, and afterward. Your plan should also incorporate points along the way at which you assess progress to date and make any necessary amendments. Leave room to add extra stages, if necessary. Remember, it won't always be possible to execute each step perfectly. Concentrate on fulfilling each point and keep a record of what you do and the results.

Breaking it down into steps

First, analyze and understand the job itself and its significance in your organization. Next map out the steps of your strategy for filling it: where you will publicize the vacancy, what support you will need to screen and rank incoming resumes, how to define your shortlist, the kinds of questions to be asked of candidates at interview, and selecting any other measures that would be required to supplement the interviews. Then there will be logistics issues to be worked out, such as where the interviews will be held.

SOLICIT EMPLOYEE REFERRALS

Reward employees for recommending friends and relatives for jobs in your organization. The new employee gets recognition, and the organization gets a well-recommended new employee.

Budgeting for your strategy

Know what your budget is from the start; finances play a role in identifying top, secondary, and optional priorities on your checklist. One key spend is likely to be on recruitment advertising. Hiring a venue for interviews and getting expert help to assess candidates' skills may also mean spending some money. Get estimates on every expenditure before you spend anything.

✔ CHECKLIST **PRE-INTERVIEW PLANNING**

	YES	NO
• Do I understand the job and where it fits in my organization?	☐	☐
• Have I planned a recruitment/interview/assessment budget?	☐	☐
• Have I decided whether supplementary meetings such as assessment centers are necessary?	☐	☐
• Have I placed the recruitment advertisements in appropriate media?	☐	☐
• Have I considered meeting places and venues for interviews?	☐	☐
• Have I designed the questions?	☐	☐
• Have I decided on the interview format (panel or pair, for example)?	☐	☐
• Have I worked in reassessment times to look back at what I have accomplished to date and consider what needs to be done next?	☐	☐

Creating the job description

The job profile starts by acting as a sort of recipe for the person you are looking for, but comes to define expectations of the job holder as well as aspects of your organization's purpose. The profile reveals one individual piece of how your organization sees its future.

TIP

LOOK AHEAD
Make sure the job description gives the role context in terms of the organization and the types of challenges and growth opportunities provided.

Setting the "rules of the game"

A well thought out job description can help to attract candidates who are right for the job. It also serves as a foundation for appraisals and employee development plans, and it outlines for both job holder and manager the "rules of the game" in day-to-day activities and over the long term. The person specification, which is often part of the job description, defines the kinds of education, experience, skills, and personal characteristics that are likely to be necessary to succeed in the job.

? ASK YOURSELF...
WHAT ARE THE JOB REQUIREMENTS

- Why does this job exist?
- What must this job holder achieve for the organization?
- Which responsibilities could be reallocated to allow the addition of new ones?
- What changes are planned for the organization that could affect this job?
- What skills should the job holder have to make the organizational transition easier?

Analyzing your needs

You may be filling an existing job that has just been vacated. A vacancy provides an opportunity to consider the continuing need for the job. If a need remains, then examine whether the role demands the inclusion of new responsibilities, competencies, and knowledge. Keep in mind that as organizations evolve, their needs and strategy change, and so must the dimensions of the work and the jobs created to carry out that work. Think about how your organization is changing and how changes impact the role.

Defining the job's purpose

The starting point for both creating and refreshing a job description or profile is defining the job's purpose. What is the main reason for the job's existence and what is the job holder expected to achieve? From there, go on to construct the description's skeleton, which must include the following: job title, main duties and responsibilities, who the job holder reports to, who reports to the job holder, where the job is based, and whether it is full-time, part-time, or flexi-time. Use the profile to build a compelling case for the job's desirability, such as responsibility for certain projects.

Sharing the full picture

Since one of the job description's purposes is to attract applicants, it can be tempting to exaggerate the most interesting aspects of the role and downplay the least interesting. Misrepresenting the job role does no one any favors. Highlight the job's best points, but balance the description so that applicants understand the full picture of what the role entails. Be truthful, skip the jargon, and write as clear and concise a description as possible.

Creating the person specification

Developing a precise person specification requires an in-depth understanding of the competencies, knowledge, skills, experience, education, aptitudes, and attitudes that the best possible selected hire for this role could have. Break requirements down into "essential" and "desirable" categories, which can help to differentiate between candidates when the time comes to build your shortlist. Focus on qualitative aspects of experience instead of an arbitrary number of years or qualifications. Perhaps the most challenging part of creating the person specification is effectively building in personal characteristics that are desirable or necessary in the job holder. Recognize that you will need to link interview questions to the person specification, as well as the job description, so consider also how a candidate can best demonstrate to you that they have, for instance, "integrity" or "initiative." Never use terms that are discriminatory, such as "mature," "bright, young graduate," and so on.

7 EXPLAIN SPECIAL CONDITIONS
List conditions such as working unusual shifts or on public holidays, regular travel, or wearing a particular uniform.

6 DESCRIBE THE SCOPE OF THE JOB
Explain the boundaries of the job holder's responsibilities and the potential for developing them further.

1 **DEFINE THE JOB PURPOSE**
Ask yourself what is the person filling this role supposed to accomplish. This step influences the rest of the process.

2 **IDENTIFY THE JOB TITLE**
The job's purpose sets out what the role should be called. Keep the job title jargon free, brief, and as clear as possible.

Developing a job profile to fit your requirements

3 **DESCRIBE THE CONTEXT**
Refer to the work conditions and nature of the business in which the job duties will be carried out.

4 **OUTLINE THE JOB'S OBJECTIVES**
Specify the key goals: for example, provide efficient customer service that ensures problems are dealt with effectively.

5 **SET OUT THE BASICS OF THE JOB**
Outline the day-to-day responsibilities and tasks, the skills needed to fulfill the job duties, and hours required weekly.

Using digital aids

Interviewing is a person-to-person interaction. However, technology can be a valuable ally in today's recruitment process. You can put technology to work for you early on to advertise your job via your corporate website or on job boards. Then well-chosen recruitment software can help to screen and organize the field of candidates who apply.

Maximizing your brand

Your organization's website is often the first port of call for two sets of job seekers. The first group knows of your organization and is interested in finding out what it would be like to work there and if there are currently any vacancies. The second is taking a look after seeing an advertisement for the job on offer. If your organization has the resources, its site should offer a careers section that features full job/person descriptions and on-line tools that allow candidates to upload resumes. Some organizations upload videos of current employees explaining what it is like to work there on their sites. Other organizations showcase written testimonials and photographs. If you can't afford "bells and whistles," ensure as a minimum that it is easy to find up-to-date job listings on the site.

TAP INTO SOCIAL MEDIA
Build your own profile on a professional social media networking site to help attract potential candidates.

Using social media

Going on-line takes your recruitment effort into a whole new cyber realm. Savvy managers and recruiters turn to professional social networking sites like LinkedIn and XING to reach "passive" job seekers (those who are not looking for jobs at the moment) and to spread the word that a job is available. To get the most out of such sites, join subgroups that can broaden your outreach—by location, industry, or profession.

Using job boards

The use of on-line job boards* as a recruitment tool for all kinds of jobs is increasing rapidly. The general job board may be the right vehicle to get the word out about entry-level and less specialized roles, but career professionals tend to seek out the niche job boards. Although job boards specializing in vacancies for senior executives are growing in popularity, they do not attract as much interest from qualified applicants as on-line services that are aimed at more junior professionals. You may want to post your vacancy on more than one job board to increase its visibility.

*__Job board__—an on-line service on which employers can post details of vacancies for a fee.

Tracking candidates

TIP

Depending on your organization's size and the number of people hired each year, software that helps to manage the recruitment process from beginning to end may be a worthwhile investment. Widely known as applicant tracking systems (ATS), recruitment software can deliver services from posting job notices and importing candidates' on-line job applications to screening resumes, scheduling interviews, managing communications with individual candidates, and more.

KNOW YOUR OPTIONS
Investigate a variety of recruitment software. Systems have been created specifically for large or small organizations.

CASE STUDY

Streamlining applications
British airline bmi increased the number of job applications it handled over a six-month period by 25 percent by putting into place recruitment and talent management software. The airline often received hundreds of applications a week, but had only a few employees working in its recruitment department.

Paperwork constituted a major part of the team's workload because applicants would first send in a resume, and would then be sent an application form. The company saved considerable costs in printing and postage by taking its application process on-line. The on-line system also made the screening of candidates more efficient.

Creating a matrix

Interviewing can become a very subjective process because it involves people, and their impressions and interpretations of information and how it is delivered. You can remove some of the subjectivity by building a framework that gives context to the relative importance of candidates' education, experience, skills, and key personal qualities.

Constructing a filtering matrix

Devising a matrix to filter the flow of candidates in the early stage of selection will save processing time. It consists of a list of candidates running down one side, and a list of minimum and preferred educational, professional experience and skills requirements running along the top. The requirements listed on the matrix should match those in the job posting. A simple "yes/no" or check system is best for indicating whether or not the requirements have been met. Ultimately, the filtering matrix is the document supporting the decision to interview, or not interview, a particular candidate.

Charting a qualitative matrix

DEVELOP A POINT SYSTEM

Decide before the actual interviews what different scores will mean in your interviewing matrix. For instance, if the top score for a given area is five, what must a candidate demonstrate to be scored at five?

An interview will require you to score candidates on information that is less factual and more qualitative in nature, so a matrix for this stage will reflect the quality of a response rather than a simple yes or no. The areas you measure will be personal qualities such as communication skills, business awareness, and knowledge. Each will receive points with, say, a top score of five. You may want to "weight" particular areas, either by raising the top score or by multiplying the given score by a number to reflect that area's importance to the hiring decision. You can use the same basic visual framework design as the filtering matrix.

Adding it all up

Organize your matrices so that information is easily accessible and your scoring system for each is easily understandable. Then create a single score sheet that outlines the accumulated score from each activity of the interviewing process for each candidate. Once you have completed interviewing and assessing your candidates, add up the scores to see which candidate has come out on top. If a question arises over selection later on, a transparent system will support and clarify your decision and the process used to make your choice.

TIP

EXAMINE ALL AREAS

Keep in mind that if you incorporate complex activities in your interview process, an additional matrix will be necessary to reflect candidates' performance there as well.

Sample of a qualitative matrix

SCORING SYSTEM:
1—No evidence of competency
2—Limited competency (one example)
3—Acceptable (meets the minimum standard for the job)
4—Significant (examples demonstrate confidence)
5—Extensive (many excellent examples that reflect
   well-rounded professional knowledge and expertise)

CANDIDATES	COMMUNICATION SKILLS	INDUSTRY KNOWLEDGE	TECHNICAL KNOWLEDGE	REGIONAL KNOWLEDGE	TOTAL SCORE
Candidate 1	3	3	3	3	12
Candidate 2	5	4	4	5	18
Candidate 3	2	3	3	4	12
Candidate 4	4	5	5	3	17

Deciding on the agenda

To make the most of your interview, you need a plan that sets out not only the informational ground you want to cover, but also outlines the time you want to devote to each segment of the interview. Your agenda should also include any "extras" that the interview process must incorporate.

Bringing the elements together

The question-and-answer segment of getting to know your candidates is referred to as "the interview," but to get the most out of your exposure to them, think instead of the interview as a multipart event that may require several different settings and techniques. The core points to decide are whether you will have a single interview or first and second interviews, and if supplementary activities should be included. For example, when candidates come in for interviews, a tour of your facility may be appropriate to give them an idea of what the work environment is like and to show them employee facilities. It will also give you a chance to see their spontaneous reactions to the environment.

Organizing your time

BUILD IN IN-BETWEEN TIME

Pleasantries take time, so be sure to plan in enough time to welcome each candidate as they come in, and tell a departing candidate good-bye and when they might expect to hear from you next.

How long each interview should last will depend on the amount of information you must obtain from each candidate. This will be based on the complexity of the role or the seniority of the position. However, you should allow at least 45–60 minutes for the question-and-answer portion of an in-person interview. Reviewing the job description and person specifications is a good starting point for developing the questions. Use it also to plan the pace of your interview by deciding how much time should be devoted to each segment, based on its importance to your selection criteria.

Planning for contingencies

The best-laid plans can go awry when the unexpected occurs. Your interviews could be thrown off kilter by late arrivals, office emergencies, or any number of everyday events. Work out a "Plan B" to help you and your candidates navigate smoothly through any problems that could occur on the day of the interview. One common contingency is running behind schedule, which can threaten the goodwill of your remaining candidates throughout the day, as well as raise the possibility that you won't get all the information you want during the interview. Perhaps the room you've arranged as the interview location has been double-booked. A candidate, or you, could be faced with a personal emergency. Develop a list of "what ifs" in order to plan effective solutions for a range of contingencies.

Building the shortlist

The list of candidates who will be invited to the interview will form your shortlist. Following the interview, you may trim this list even further to choose some to participate in further selection activities in your search for the best possible candidate.

Selecting the best

Build your interview shortlist with the help of the filtering matrix, which will make it clear which applicants met most of your requirements and which did not. Your next steps depend on two factors: how many applicants met most or all of the minimum and preferred requirements, and how many people you want to interview for the job. If your list does not include the desired number of candidates to interview, look at the applicants who met the highest percentage of the minimum requirements. Examine their resumes for individual differentiators, such as evidence of promotions, recent training, or unpaid work experience.

Achieving a manageable shortlist

Work with at least one other person to develop your shortlist to eliminate the possibility of bias. For a manageable list, keep in mind how much time you will have to devote to interviews. A shortlist for a senior or complex role should be small, because there will be few people with the right blend of skills, experience, and personal qualities who meet highly specific requirements. Too many applicants for a high-level role means that the job posting may have been written too broadly.

If you are hiring in volume, consider initial telephone screening to help you narrow your shortlist to interview. Telephone screening can also be useful for confirming the candidates' credentials, probing gaps in employment history, exploring their willingness to relocate, or determining whether their salary expectations are in line with what your organization is prepared to offer. Telephone screening can save money and time by eliminating unqualified or inappropriate applicants from the shortlist to interview.

TIP

USE MULTIPLE SHORTLISTS

Consider ranking the candidates in separate categories, based on key priorities for the job—for example, professional skill, management experience, and education—and invite the top two in each list for the interview.

Considering the overqualified

As a recruiting manager you may face the difficult task of deciding whether a job will sufficiently challenge and stimulate a potential employee. Some organizations look unfavorably on overqualified candidates, because of concerns that they might get bored or that they will cost too much. Other employers look at hiring such candidates as an opportunity to develop a role and, possibly, a team or the entire organization in new ways. If you have seemingly overqualified applicants on your shortlist, ask yourself what their impact would be in a particular job role.

Inviting the candidates

Extend the invitation to a job interview with the same enthusiasm with which you hope your candidates receive it. Be clear in the information you provide, and prepare to adapt your plans if some candidates require special assistance.

TIP

ADDRESS WITH CARE

Address candidates by first names instead of Mr. or Ms. initially, to avoid embarrassment over gender-neutral names.

Personalizing the invitation

An invitation to attend an interview is the first personalized communication you will send a candidate, and it must accomplish several things: provide information, get across a sense of your organization's style and culture, and communicate pleasure that the candidate has chosen to apply for this role. Using phrases like "I am pleased to invite you," "We look forward to meeting you," or "Your experience interested us greatly" will personalize the tone of your communication, whether delivered by phone, letter, or email. Telephone the candidate to discuss and agree on a time, and then send your letter or email to confirm the arrangement.

IN FOCUS...
PRE-INTERVIEW QUESTIONNAIRES

One of the world's most influential experts on recruitment, Dr. John Sullivan, recommends that managers give candidates a series of questions to answer before an interview to save valuable time and to help interviewers find out more about them beforehand. Candidates might be asked about job preferences, career goals, and motivators, for instance, in questionnaires that are sent to them with the interview invitation and returned before the interview. Such questionnaires could be given only to those candidates who are selected for interview, but Sullivan suggests that they could also be used to screen out a few applicants from that pool.

Providing the right information

Considering special needs

The invitation sent to candidates must detail the date, time, and place the interview will be held. Send a map or a weblink to a map of the area so that they can find the venue easily. Also say who will conduct the interview. Let them know if they need to bring passports, work portfolios, or other documents or materials. Provide advice on how to reschedule their interviews if the given time and date are not convenient. Also give names and contact details, such as cell phone numbers so that they can let you know if they have been delayed on the interview day.

When inviting candidates to interviews, ask if they have any particular requirements. These could include:
• making the venue easily accessible if a candidate has mobility problems.
• allowing for or providing an interpreter for hearing- or speech-impaired candidates.
• allowing a friend or relative to accompany a candidate to support or help them.
• providing equipment to help sight impaired candidates read any necessary material.
• offering a break midinterview.

ISSUING INVITATION LETTERS

FAST TRACK

OFF TRACK

FAST TRACK	OFF TRACK
Addressing the communication to the candidate by name	Sending an interview invitation to "Dear Applicant"
Providing contact names and phone numbers for the interview date in case the candidate has an emergency	Offering no way to contact you on the day of the interview if a candidate has a problem
Taking a proactive approach to adapting interview conditions for candidates with special needs	Telling special needs candidates that they will have to experience the same interview conditions as everyone else

Chapter 2

Conducting the interview

The interview is the first opportunity for you to get to know the person behind the resume, so every element is extremely important. Keep in mind that the interview will also shape the candidate's impression of your organization.

Setting the tone

When you go to a live performance of a play, from the moment the curtain goes up, the scenery, the backdrop, and the background music give you clues as to what you are about to experience. The same is true for your candidates as soon as they arrive for the interview.

REMOVE DISTRACTIONS

Leave behind communications tools—office phones, cell phones, and PDAs such as BlackBerrys—or keep them turned off.

Selecting a venue

If you have chosen a neutral location such as a hotel as an interview venue, it is best to host your interviews in a comparatively formal setting, such as a suite or conference room instead of a lobby or restaurant where too many distractions await. Similarly, if you hold the interviews at your own premises, book a private room or office so that your meetings with candidates will be free from distractions such as phone calls and other interruptions. Check in advance that the setting is neat and does not have personal items such as inappropriate calendars or posters in view.

Getting to the right place

Make sure that your candidates know where they should go on arrival and who they will see for the interview—these basic details will help them begin the process with confidence. A further boost to the candidates' confidence will come when their first contact welcomes them at the meeting point. Then a comfortable, pleasant place to wait for their interview will suggest that your organization is well organized and committed to seeing candidates begin interviews in the most relaxed state possible.

MAKE THE VENUE ACCESSIBLE

Do your best not to send candidates on their own on complicated routes around floors of offices that will look all the same to them—appoint an escort to guide them.

Meeting the candidate

Bring with you the candidate's resume and any other relevant material: the questions you will ask, the job and person specifications, organizational background, and a notepad and pen. When you meet them, offer a warm, professional greeting, using their name, and provide a glass of water. Some small talk about the weather or their trip to the premises is appropriate.

BE ON TIME

Be punctual—keeping the candidate waiting without a genuine emergency reflects poorly on your organization.

✔ CHECKLIST PREPARING FOR A CANDIDATE

	YES	NO
• Is your meeting place free from distractions and interruptions?	☐	☐
• Is the candidate aware of where they need to go?	☐	☐
• Do the relevant people, such as a receptionist or security personnel, know that the candidate is coming and where they are to be taken?	☐	☐
• Did you bring the candidate's resume and other relevant materials, such as a list of the questions to be asked?	☐	☐
• Are drinking water and cups accessible nearby?	☐	☐
• Do you know how to pronounce the candidate's name?	☐	☐

Choosing the format

The format of the interview provides a framework for its content. Issues to consider include whether the interview should be conducted one-on-one or two-on-one, or if a panel is required. Circumstances may even dictate that the interview takes place on the telephone or by video conferencing.

Interviewing with a panel

To select a candidate for a very senior, highly technical, or otherwise multifaceted position, interviewing by panel may be the most effective option. A clear structure, so that the interview flows and each panel member knows what they are responsible for, is essential to a successful panel interview. So is having a lead or primary interviewer to guide the interview's direction. The secondary panelists can offer clarifying questions and provide additional thoughts later. But remember to limit the numbers—more than four panelists may overwhelm and confuse your candidates.

Teaming up

Most first-stage interviews involve one or two interviewers. Asking questions, listening to and recording answers, observing, and then deciding to either hire the candidate or move on to the next stage of selection is a lot for one person. During the interview, two interviewers can alternate between asking questions and taking notes. Later, two sets of observations and insights are likely to be more helpful toward building a complete picture of a candidate's suitability for a role.

Interviewing at a distance

Distance may make a face-to-face interview impractical. If telephone manner and customer service are significant parts of the job, it would make sense to have a first interview by phone. If you can use a video linkup, the interview will be much the same to conduct as if it were in person. If interviewing by telephone, speak distinctly and keep in mind that it will be even more important to convey warmth and professionalism in your voice. Try smiling naturally as you speak, so that it can be heard in your voice and choose a quiet place away from distractions and interruptions.

TIP

TEST THE TECHNOLOGY

Leave time to check that the video-conferencing equipment is working before you begin an interview. If it fails, you will waste time tracking down a technician to make it work.

ASK YOURSELF... HOW SHOULD I CHOOSE AN INTERVIEW FORMAT?

- How complex is the job role?
- At what stage do we need to see the candidate in person?
- What resources are available to conduct an effective distance interview?
- Who else from my organization should be involved in the interviews?
- What will I look to a fellow interviewer to deliver?
- How would we structure a panel interview?

Competency-based questions

The goal of the interviewing process is to find the right candidate who will bring the right skills to the job. Asking candidates to explain how and when they have used the precise competencies in past experiences and situations will give you insight as to their suitability for the job.

Understanding competency

The idea behind competency-based questions is to link past behavior and experiences with the skills needed for the job and future performance. These questions are also known as behavioral questions. Instead of asking what a person would do in a given situation, the interviewer asks candidates to describe how they have handled such a situation previously. This kind of questioning is seen by many professionals as the most reliable, because past performance is the best predictor of how a person will perform in the future.

Using the STAR method

The STAR method can guide you through the dual responsibilities of preparing competency questions, and then listening effectively to candidates' responses. STAR is an acronym that stands for Situation, Task, Action, Response. First, outline the type of situation you want the candidates to refer back to in your questions. When a candidate responds, you are listening for a description of a situation that matches the requirements you outlined in the question, a logical approach to solving the problem, specific actions taken to address the challenge, as well as clear results.

"Describe a situation in which you worked with another department."

"Give an example of a time when you had to work with a difficult customer."

"Tell me how you handled a situation in which you had to make a quick decision without having all of the facts."

"Tell me about a time when you had to motivate your team under difficult circumstances."

Assessing competency

"Give an example of how you managed a particularly demanding project."

"This job requires 10 days of travel every month. Describe the travel requirements of a previous job, and how you dealt with the challenges."

"Please give an example of how you dealt with interpersonal conflict in your team."

"Describe a situation in which you handled conflicting requests from senior managers."

Asking further questions

A clear picture of each candidate's experience and background should emerge from interviews. While competency-based questions should deliver most of the "meat" from your interviews, you will want to obtain information from candidates that may require other types of questions.

VALUE TIME

While asking verification questions, be careful not to waste valuable interview time by asking candidates to recite their resumes to you word-for-word.

Verifying credentials

Exploring the credentials and past experience that candidates have cited on their resumes is an important part of interviewing. Basic verification questions would cover factual aspects of their education and experience, such as "How long did you attend that school?", and "Which courses did you take?" To obtain more value-based information about their education or experience, ask questions such as: "What motivated you to seek higher education?", and "How did you juggle school work with working at a part-time job?" Verification questions allow you to check for gaps that could tip you off to an untruth or exaggeration in their list of credentials.

ENCOURAGE STORYTELLING

To ensure fairness, you will be asking each of the candidates the same questions, but prepare to ask follow-up questions to clarify candidates' responses or prompt greater detail.

Diversifying your approach

Open questions, such as "Tell me about yourself," give your candidates a chance to list their skills and experiences to the requirements of the job. If you are seeking factual information, a closed question will be appropriate, for example, "How many staff did you manage?" Probing questions could also be described as follow-on questions because they are likely to follow a response and are intended to encourage the candidate to explain their answer in detail. Unorthodox or unusual questions may prompt intriguing answers, but be certain you know what you want to achieve by asking such a question that, on the surface, has little to do with the job at hand. Questions such as "What is your favorite film and why?" can inject a light moment into an interview, or they can offer some insight into a candidate's passions and creativity. Stress questions, on the other hand, are designed to reveal how a candidate reacts to pressurized questions. However, introducing added stress into an already stressful interview may be counterproductive!

USING DIFFERENT TYPES OF QUESTION

QUESTION TYPE	EXAMPLE	IMPACT
Open	"Tell us about yourself."	Allows candidates to match skills or experiences to the job
Closed	"How many new offices have you opened?"	Secures a brief, specific answer
Hypothetical/ situational	"What would you do if…"	Assesses how candidates think on their feet and gives insight into their priorities and judgment
Probing	"Could you elaborate on how you achieved that result under those circumstances?"	Follow-up questions that are intended to draw out more information
Verification	"Can you confirm when and where you completed your health and safety certification?"	Similar to a closed question; seeking brief answers to verify and confirm factual information
Leading	"Part of the job is publishing a monthly newsletter. Have you done this before?"	Intended to secure a "yes" or "no" answer with further elaboration by the candidate
Stress	"If you were on a plane that was going to crash, who would you save—yourself, your boss, or your mother?"	An aggressive form of questioning that puts the candidate under stress to see how they will react
Unusual/quirky	"If you were a vegetable, what would you want to be and why?"	Aimed at eliciting information about a candidate's creativity and how they think

Respecting diversity

Having a diverse workforce begins with recruiting men and women of different races, religions, nationalities, ages, and sexual orientation into the organization— and the interview is the first step to achieving this.

Attracting diversity

To attract the widest variety of employees possible, reflect the presence of diversity in your organization in all of your on-line and print recruitment materials. Improving interviewing skills is important to finding the right person—but it is also important to remember that the successful candidate can either be a man or a woman and come from varied backgrounds, ages, lifestyles, and life situations.

EMPLOYEE ASSOCIATIONS
Be aware of employee associations that your organization sponsors for members of different ethnic groups or religions, or if it supports special interest groups.

Recognizing differences

If your candidate pool is diverse, cultural awareness will be essential during your interviews—both to understand how candidates present themselves and how you respond. A smile and a pleasant manner go a long way toward bridging cultural gaps anywhere around the world. Insure that your interview protocol reflects a positive attitude toward diversity— from your welcome, to the questions you ask and your body language.

CORPORATE DRESSING
Check if your organization's policy on corporate dress or grooming allows adaptation for different religious requirements for both men and women.

Addressing candidates' cultural concerns

GESTURES AND EYE CONTACT
Understand that a handshake may not be appropriate between men and women, and extended eye contact can signify anger in some cultures.

RELIGIOUS FACILITIES
Find out if there are facilities onsite for prayer or rituals during the day, and check the organization's policy on time off during religious observances.

EATING HABITS
See if the cafeteria offers vegetarian, kosher, and halal dishes, and if office refrigerators have separate shelves for vegetarian and meat dishes.

Avoiding illegal questions

You may want to ask certain questions to ensure that a candidate is the right choice for your organization. As you see it, you are probing the candidate's suitability for the job. But recognize that many questions may be not only inappropriate, but illegal.

Understanding the playing field

Laws vary from country to country regarding which questions are illegal to ask job applicants, and who can or can't work in a country. To avoid legal difficulties, consult your organization's employment legal adviser. You might find it difficult to assess what is appropriate to ask candidates, but one rule of thumb is that if the question you want to ask refers to a candidate's personal life and not specifically to a job requirement, it is probably inappropriate to ask.

Asking the right question

Think about what you really want to know about when you consider asking personal questions such as "Which country are you from?"; "Are you planning to have children?"; "What religion are you?"; or "How old are you?" If you believe a candidate's national origin is important, what you probably need to know is, "Do you have a legal right to work in this country?" Your interest in a candidate's family plans may reflect your need to know if they are willing to travel, as the job requires. Instead of asking about a candidate's religion, the relevant issue may be whether they are willing to work particular hours and days of the week. Rather than asking about a candidate's age, pinpoint the issue at the root of the question: is the person physically capable of carrying a certain amount of weight necessary for the job?

Avoiding a wrong move

Using the interview to develop a personal relationship with a candidate is out of bounds. In show business, the phrase "the casting couch" refers to the practice of turning auditions, or interviews, into opportunities to leverage relationships with performers or with authority figures. Business has also suffered from the occasional scandal when a gatekeeper*, such as an interviewer, initiates or accepts inappropriate overtures. During the interview, you and the candidate may discover a common interest that both of you wish to pursue outside the business environment. However, pursuing a relationship—no matter how innocent—as a result of the interview could lead your organization's management to question your judgment on candidate selection. It could also lead to legal and reputation difficulties for you and your organization. Avoid it at all costs.

*Gatekeeper—a person who controls access of people, commodities, or information to an organization or to the public.

NAVIGATING LEGAL ISSUES

FAST TRACK	OFF TRACK
Asking which languages they know	Asking where they were born
Asking if they are willing to relocate	Asking if they are married
Asking if they would be able to carry out all the job responsibilities	Asking if their religion allows them to do a certain type of work
Asking if they belong to any professional associations that are relevant to the job	Asking which kinds of social, religious, or political groups they belong to
Offering a glass of water before and during the interview	Inviting them out for a coffee on a personal basis

Effective observation

The point of the interview is to gather as much information as possible about the candidates who have applied for a particular job. To obtain this information, you must ask questions, and then listen carefully to the answers. Visual observation of the candidates is also important.

TIP

BE PATIENT

Fight the urge to interrupt or finish interviewees' sentences; be comfortable with a certain amount of silence before moving on to the next point.

Listening actively

Focus on what the candidate is saying, by both listening to the words and observing changing vocal tone, volume, and pace. If you are taking notes, listen for key ideas from the candidate's answer—don't try to write down every word they say. When the candidate has finished responding, ensure that you have understood by summarizing one or two of the key points back to them. Then gather more information by asking the candidate to clarify or elaborate their response.

Communicating nonverbally

Your nonverbal cues can either reinforce or contradict the interview's stated purpose. For example, encouraging a candidate verbally to "Tell me about yourself" while fiddling with a paperclip sends conflicting messages. Sitting back in your chair with arms folded can be taken to mean that you are sceptical of what they are saying, and suggest a closed mind, even if that is not how you actually feel. Checking your watch can be interpreted as a desire for the meeting to be over. On the other hand, leaning forward as the candidate speaks, maintaining eye contact, smiling, and occasionally nodding to acknowledge that you are taking on board what they say, lets interviewees know that you are engaged.

Nonverbal clues

When you observe the candidate during the interview, you too are looking for signs of engagement. The ability to listen and an interest in the job at hand are among the first requirements. Also look for nonverbal clues to character, ability to interact with others, confidence, and other traits that would affect a candidate's future success in the job. Physical gestures such as head nods and hand movements can suggest interest in a conversation or a particular topic. Other body movements, such as finger or foot tapping or leg swinging can reflect discomfort, perhaps boredom, or tension. Inappropriate laughter can be a sign of nerves. Be sure to write down what you observe.

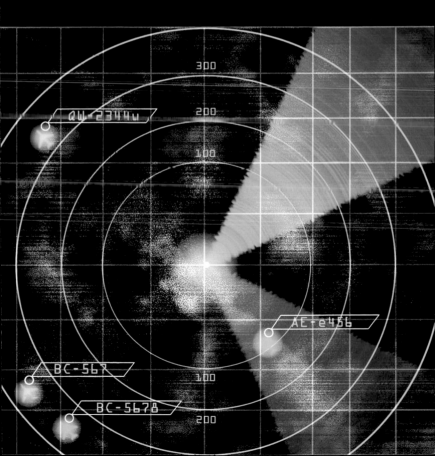

Concluding the interview

You have explored your candidate's resume, explained the job and person specification, and gained insight into the skills and knowledge that they would bring to the job. Now it is time to end the meeting. Bringing the interview to a successful close will help both candidate and interviewer move seamlessly into the next stage of the recruitment process.

TIP

GAUGE INTEREST
Post-interview, gauge a candidate's interest in the role by their enthusiasm and the eagerness they show in any follow-up.

Questioning the interviewer

When you have finished asking the questions, ask the candidate to offer any additional information they have not covered that is relevant to the job. Also invite them to ask any questions they have. Be prepared to answer questions about the impact of current events on your organization. If your organization has been in the news recently, candidates may want to ask you about the issues involved. The candidate who has researched your organization before the interview should know what your organization does, but you should be ready to answer any questions that they may have about the organization's plans for growth, diversification, or consolidation, and how the job on offer fits into a long-term strategy. This stage may well be too early to discuss salary and benefits, but come prepared to respond to such a question, even if it is only to say, "We will discuss those points at a later date." After they have asked their questions, ask the candidates if the job still interests them and whether they would like to proceed to the next stage.

Q IN FOCUS...
KEEPING THE END MOVING

Be alert to signs that the candidate suspects that the interview has not gone well, and that they are going to try to make up for any miscommunication in the last few minutes of the interview. If a candidate wants to return to a particular response to one of your questions or clarify a point, you could gain additional insight that will be helpful to your decision. However, letting them overexplain with no real point is helpful to no one. Know when it's time to cut the talk short.

Moving forward

The candidate will also want to know what will happen next. Be as open and clear as possible about the process ahead. If you plan to hire someone based on the first round of interviews, say so. If you will be conducting second interviews, skills tests, or an assessment center, tell them. If you are basing your choice purely on the interviews, let them know the date by which you expect to have made a decision. Likewise, if you plan second-stage meetings, provide the candidate with as much information as possible about when they will be notified if their application is being taken forward and when the next round of selection will begin. You should also be as open as possible about when they will know if their application has not been successful.

Tidying up loose ends

Closing out a job interview should leave both parties feeling that the meeting fulfilled their goals; the candidates should feel they have successfully communicated to you their suitability for the role, or alternatively that the role is not right for them. As the interviewer, you should feel that you have obtained all the information needed at the current stage of the recruitment process. You should also feel that you have a good idea of whether the candidate matches the job and person specifications closely enough to progress further to the next selection round. Housekeeping details that require attending to at the end include ensuring that the address, email, and phone number you have on file for the candidate will remain current through the next stage of the selection process. Thank them for coming, and offer a smile and a handshake—if appropriate—to end the meeting.

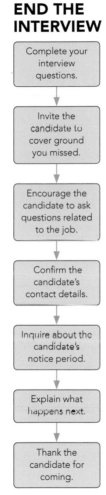

HOW TO...
END THE
INTERVIEW

Complete your interview questions.

↓

Invite the candidate to cover ground you missed.

↓

Encourage the candidate to ask questions related to the job.

↓

Confirm the candidate's contact details.

↓

Inquire about the candidate's notice period.

↓

Explain what happens next.

↓

Thank the candidate for coming.

Chapter 3

Supplementing the interview

An interview may not be enough to fully gauge your shortlisted candidates' capabilities, on-the-job potential, and suitability for a particular role. Even after an in-depth interview, you will need the help of additional tools to find out more about the candidate.

Gathering further information

No matter how well planned, the basic interview does not guarantee that a complete picture will emerge of how well a candidate fits all the requirements of a given role. Background information is required, and you may have to seek help from professionals to make the right decision.

KNOW THE LEGAL REQUIREMENTS

Some jobs may have mandatory minimum qualifications prescribed by law. Make sure you are aware of any requirements for the job under offer.

Uncovering skills

Resumes and interviews are vehicles for candidates to "tell" what they can do and what they have done. However, they don't allow them to actually "show" their aptitude for certain competencies required. Nor do they let candidates demonstrate how they would perform in a typical work scenario. In jobs requiring high levels of skill, for example, it may be necessary to verify that candidates actually have the required special skills. Depending on the job's complexity, various kinds of tests and activities can be done to uncover a candidate's professional skills, ability, and aptitude.

Establishing background

In some cases, the sensitive nature of some jobs—such as working with children or hazardous chemicals—may dictate examination of the candidates' backgrounds to confirm that they are suitable for a role. Since new technology offers opportunities to investigate the ways in which people put themselves forward to friends, family, and colleagues, you can now take other steps to make sure candidates are a good organizational fit.

Using professional assessment

Expert assistance will probably be required to help you conduct most of the in-depth assessments to ensure that you select the best person for the job. Ask your HR director to recommend assessment professionals. You can even consult psychologists and test publishers. But regardless of your consultant's knowledge, it is your responsibility to understand what information you need to know about each candidate—this will arm your experts with the knowledge to create the most effective tools in obtaining this information.

PLAN YOUR STRATEGY

Work with your expert consultants to decide the supplemental assessments needed before you advertise the role. Then you can advise candidates about the breadth of the selection process.

ASK YOURSELF... WHAT MORE DO I NEED TO KNOW?

- Are there specific personal characteristics that are needed in the job?
- Which hard competencies are required—for example, typing, standard office software, numeracy, proficiency in a foreign language, or data checking?
- How well would the candidate interact with clients or deliver a presentation?
- Will I want to verify past employment, qualifications or, in some cases, immigration status and right to work in my country?
- Does the job require working with vulnerable people such as children?
- How do the candidates represent themselves to professional and personal peers?

Holding an assessment center

To test for job-specific skills, capabilities, and personal traits, you may want to hold an assessment center. The term "assessment center" doesn't refer to a specific place; it is a series of exercises designed to reveal candidates' personal characteristics, capabilities, skills, and potential to succeed in the job you are filling.

INCLUDE A SOCIAL EVENT

Hosting a reception or lunch for your candidates will allow you to see how they respond to others away from the assessment environment.

Matching tests and roles

The assessment center is your opportunity to scrutinize candidates against the selection criteria you outlined in the job description and person specification. In addition to measuring job skills, an assessment center also requires candidates to adapt to a variety of different challenges under the watchful eyes of qualified assessors who observe their behavior while they perform tasks and participate in activities. The nature of the exercises and activities included will depend on the type of job to be filled and should require candidates to demonstrate the skills and abilities that they would actually need on the job.

GIVE FEEDBACK

Be sure that feedback on performance is offered to all participants—they need to know which traits or skills the assessments flagged up as meeting or not meeting the job requirements.

Planning exercises

At a typical assessment center, exercises might include: online or paper-and-pencil tests to assess personality, aptitude, and skills; exercises based on day-to-day work situations; interviews; role-play and simulation scenarios; presentations; and group activities. For more senior and complex roles, the exercises may take several days. The event could be held at your organization's head office or a neutral location, such as a hotel, leased office space, or convention center. Consider how many candidates must attend when deciding how much space will be needed.

Standardizing tests

Creating an assessment center requires the involvement of experts to design the exercises and to assess candidates. Expert advice and analysis are especially needed when you want to use psychological testing in your selection process. The International Task Force on Assessment Center Guidelines underscores that training assessors is crucial to an effective assessment center. It recommends that when you are choosing assessors, take into account their knowledge and experience with similar assessment techniques, plus their familiarity with the organization and the job to be filled. You may want to train people from within your own organization as assessors, but you could also consider using professional psychologists

HOW TO...
PLAN AND RUN AN ASSESSMENT CENTER

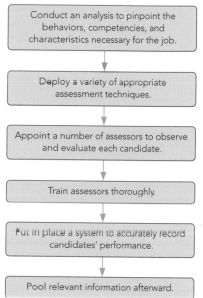

Conduct an analysis to pinpoint the behaviors, competencies, and characteristics necessary for the job.

Deploy a variety of appropriate assessment techniques.

Appoint a number of assessors to observe and evaluate each candidate.

Train assessors thoroughly.

Put in place a system to accurately record candidates' performance.

Pool relevant information afterward.

IN FOCUS... HISTORY OF MILITARY ASSESSMENT CENTERS

The purpose of assessment centres is to give an idea of how a candidate operates in a work situation. They were first used by the military to aid in the selection of officers. The German military used job simulations, along with other capability measurements, to select officers after World War I. From 1942, the British War Office adopted an officer selection system loosely based on observations of the German method. The US Office of Strategic Services ran a three-day program of tests to improve its spy selection during World War II. In each case, the intention was to discover how candidates responded to the pressures of real-life situations.

Using psychometric tests

Organizations increasingly use psychometric tests to help identify in individuals the specific characteristics, abilities, and aptitudes that are likely to predict a person's success in a particular job.

Understanding psychometrics

Psychometric tests measure psychological variables such as intelligence, aptitude, and personality traits, and they are available from credible psychometrics providers. They often involve answering multiple-choice questions, and many can be administered both off-line and on-line. Sometimes these assessments are used to develop psychological profiles of candidates, covering personality and intellectual ability. They can also be used to measure emotional intelligence, preferred work style, candidates' ability to learn, and their potential to achieve in the future. An example of a psychometric instrument is the Myers-Briggs Type Indicator. With this tool, users' responses to a series of multiple-choice questions determine which of 16 personality types they most closely match.

CONFIDENTIALITY
Only people with a legitimate "need to know" as part of the selection process should have access to results.

Choosing what to measure

A thorough study of the manual that comes with each test will help you understand the research that has been conducted to assure the particular assessment's effectiveness. Statistical information outlining its reliability, predictability, and other factors can help you decide if a particular test is right for helping you find out what you want to know.

STANDARDIZATION
The tests must be given under controlled conditions and scored using standard criteria.

Criteria for effective psychometric testing

NON-DISCRIMINATION
No group should be disadvantaged because of age, gender, disability, religion, or race.

OBJECTIVITY
The final results must not be affected by the assessors' personal beliefs, opinions, or values.

PREDICTABILITY
The test must accurately predict performance in real work as well as assessment situations.

RELIABILITY
Fundamental errors must be minimized and quantified, and taken into account when assessing results.

Testing skills and ability

Depending on the kind of job you're filling, tests that measure certain types of learned knowledge and skills may be very useful to the selection process. Tests are available to assess your candidates' abilities and aptitudes in many areas, from IT skills to spatial reasoning*.

*Spatial reasoning —the ability to visualize images, mentally move them around, and understand how their positions change with movement in one direction or another.

Testing professional skills

How do you know if candidates can do what they say they can? With certain types of professional skills, it is easy and cost effective to find out by testing for them. Today, it is possible to measure many skills using web-based tests, and it is possible to give candidates a choice as to where they take the tests—at a specified location, such as during an on-site assessment centre, at their home, or wherever there is access to the Internet.

A skill testing service will be able to provide you with myriads of tests that gauge proficiency in specific IT disciplines, foreign languages, administrative operations such as credit management, payroll and office software, industrial specialities, and virtually every kind of job in business that involves processes, technical knowledge, or data usage. Expect test scores to be accompanied by a report that analyzes the results, so that those making the hiring selection can understand candidates' individual strengths and weaknesses in depth.

IN FOCUS...
ABILITY VS. APTITUDE

The terms "ability" and "aptitude" are often used interchangeably, but various tests may differentiate between the two. Ability might be defined as an enabling proficiency, which means someone can do a particular thing, often thanks to a learned skill or qualification. Aptitude reflects more a candidate's capacity or talent to do something. Some view "ability" as the basis of aptitude, and aptitude as more job-related than ability. Another way of looking at it is to think of ability as a person's capability to do something, and aptitude as the potential to become capable of doing it.

Measuring aptitude and ability

Aptitude is more about a person's propensity for a particular type of thinking or reasoning, which is necessary to succeed in the role, than it is about a well-developed skill. For example, an individual who understands the relationship between shapes, dimensions, and space could be said to have an aptitude for spatial reasoning, the focus of some specialized aptitude tests. Abstract reasoning, or the ability to analyze information and solve problems, is another common theme of aptitude testing. Aptitude for a given discipline can be very important, particularly when filling jobs in which you expect the successful candidates to undergo future training to become qualified or proficient at the job.

In some cases, instead of measuring aptitude, you may need to get an idea of candidates' abilities to communicate and use basic arithmetic. A verbal ability test would typically cover word usage, spelling, different parts of speech, reading, and following instructions. Multiplication, division, and reading charts and graphs might be included in a numeric ability test.

CREATE YOUR OWN TESTS

Explore the possibility of building your own tests—some test suppliers offer this option, depending on the job and the skills you want to test.

CHOOSING APPROPRIATE TESTS

FAST TRACK	**OFF TRACK**
Defining which abilities and skills are needed for the job	Being unaware or doubtful about which abilities and skills are needed
Seeking out tests that will measure those skills and abilities	Believing all candidates when they say they can meet all requirements
Scrutinizing the analytical reports that should accompany the test	Considering only the overall scores on the tests

Conducting group activities

Role play and group activities offer great benefits when they are used as part of the recruitment process. Unlike psychometric and aptitude tests, these exercises give candidates a chance to put their interpersonal skills center stage and put theory into practice.

TIP

PRACTICE DISCRETION

Do take notes during group activities, but take a discreet approach so not to make participants feel that you are waiting for them to make a mistake.

Watching candidates in action

You've been getting some insight into your candidates' aptitude and personality traits—now you will see them put their skills, experience, social abilities, and work habits to use in simulated workplace events. This is where you and your assessors will have to work your hardest to observe and record actions and responses. This blend of verbal communications and body language should fill in many of the remaining blanks about your candidates—for example, their ability to work in a team, how well they think in stressful conditions, and whether they are effective listeners. Although cultural differences may affect a person's nonverbal behavior, you can often glean hints about someone's attitudes by observing basic facial expressions and body language.

Planning activities

Keep the rules simple and clear: specific time allowances must be met, the target goal of a team project must be defined, the guidelines for giving a presentation must be outlined, and the characters and scenarios to be portrayed in role-play events must be understood by the participants. The exercises must be well planned and pose genuine challenges to the participants. However, their structures must not be so complicated that participants are confused instead of stimulated.

Reading basic body language

LEANING FORWARD
Implies the person is interested in what is being said, especially if the head is also held forward.

FIDGETING
Might reflect nervousness. Examples include constantly adjusting one's clothes, or toying with nearby objects.

CROSSING ARMS OR LEGS
Can suggest defensiveness to people or the situation, but can also mean the person is feeling cold.

EYE ROLLING
Might indicate frustration, annoyance, or contempt for another person's opinion or action, even if it is done silently.

DRUMMING OR TAPPING FINGERS
Could signify a person's agitation, boredom, or impatience in a given situation.

MAINTAINING EYE CONTACT
Can mean interest in what is being said, while a fixed stare can mean the person is feigning interest.

TIP

WATCH YOUR COSTS

Use your budget on critical expenses such as the right staffing and essential exercise materials. Organizationally branded items such as paper, pens, and pencils are nice-to-haves, but won't help identify the best candidate.

Structuring the exercises

Do you want your role-play exercises to involve only your job candidates? Or do you want at least one of the roles taken on by an uninvolved player? Remember: the more candidates you involve in the exercise, the more qualified observers you will need on hand to ensure that each job applicant is carefully and equally assessed. Sometimes assessment center organizers bring in actors who are skilled in dramatic improvisation to portray other characters in role-play exercises so that observers can focus their attention on the candidates. Bringing in additional experts will boost the cost of your assessment center, which may already be expensive. However, the importance of getting the right person for the particular role or roles you are filling could justify the extra cost. An actor could also facilitate a chaired discussion, unless you would like to put a candidate in the role of chair. Putting one candidate in the role of chair can be an effective tool to assess that person's ability to facilitate a group discussion or project. However, that could lead to the participants getting the impression that the person portraying the chair is the favored candidate to get the job. Rotating candidates in and out of the chair's role may draw better performance from the group as a whole.

✔ CHECKLIST **PREPARING FOR GROUP ACTIVITIES**

	YES	NO
• Have you ordered the right activity materials?	☐	☐
• Will the space accommodate the activities you have planned?	☐	☐
• Will you have enough assessors to observe candidates effectively?	☐	☐
• Have you structured the activities clearly with goals and allotted completion times?	☐	☐
• Do the assessors know what you are looking for from each exercise?	☐	☐

CHOOSING ROLE PLAY AND GROUP ACTIVITIES

ACTIVITY	HOW IT WORKS	WHAT IT REVEALS
Leaderless discussion	Candidates are given a problem to discuss for a specific amount of time, during which they must develop solutions.	Leadership, negotiation, influencing, and verbal communication skills, creativity, and nonverbal communication style
Practical task	This is a creative problem-solving exercise that may involve constructing an object with unusual materials or by moving them around in an unusual way.	Interpersonal, teamwork, project management, and problem-solving skills
In-tray or e-tray exercise	Designed to simulate a typical workload for the person who gets the job, the exercise may include memos, budget forecasts, trend information, reports, messages, and emergencies that must be dealt with within a given amount of time.	Managerial capabilities such as organization, task prioritization, delegation, time management, and attention to detail while also being able to take a holistic view to problem solving, decision making, and planning
Oral presentation	Candidates must prepare a talk on a given topic with minimal preparation time.	Creativity, confidence, preparation, ability to think on feet, and to structure and effectively communicate a message
Role play	A scenario involving two or more people is created in which a candidate plays a specified role and deals with a specific on-the-job situation.	Communication, listening and negotiation skills, empathy, problem solving, responses to certain situations
Case study	Candidates are briefed on a typical business problem and must make recommendations.	Ability to analyze information and make decisions
Business game	Candidates working in groups compete to come up with the best solution to a business problem, such as a bankruptcy or hostile takeover bid.	Skills in teamwork, creative decision making, situational analysis

Background screening

Knowing exactly who a candidate is before you bring that person on board will be crucial to your organization's well-being. Issues such as identity, false career information, criminal pasts, and illegal immigration are important and need to be checked early on to avoid problems later.

HOW TO... CHECK OUT NEW RECRUITS

Verify their identity.

Verify academic records.

Verify professional credentials.

Check right-to-work documents.

Commission public and criminal records checks.

Consider other checks as needed.

Protecting your organization

It is obvious that an organization needs to be certain that new recruits will bring to the new job all of the education, qualifications, skills, and experience they claim to have, in order for the organization to benefit. You want to believe everything candidates say on their resumes and in interviews, and trust that they have told you everything. But strong competition for particular jobs and tightened employment standards in certain industries mean there is a greater likelihood of candidates falsifying, or omitting, necessary information from their applications. Failing to take steps to confirm candidates' identity and background can leave your organization vulnerable to a number of serious risks such as employee fraud, legal liability and litigation, theft of sensitive organization and customer information, damage to the organization's reputation, and costs stemming from negligent hiring procedures.

Deciding what you need to know

Senior-level roles, certain specialized jobs, and positions with access to sensitive information or vulnerable people may require more extensive and complex checks of candidates. You may want to outsource complicated screening to a specialized agency. But consider first which checks would be most relevant to the job, organization, and industry involved

Confirming identity

The most basic vetting procedure is to check references for past education, membership in professional organizations, and employment details that candidates have given you. However, previous employers may be reluctant to confirm details other than dates of employment because of possible legal action if the candidate does not get the job. Get candidates to help you with simple methods of confirming identity and address by having them bring in identity documents with a photograph (such as a passport or driver's license), a recent bank statement (within the last three months), and a utility bill addressed to them at their current home. Foreign candidates must provide documentation that they are currently eligible to work in your country.

TIP

AVOID DISCRIMINATION
Ask all candidates to show you their passports so that you are not singling out non-natives for travel document checks.

Using social networking sites

The Internet is used by many people to share details of their personal lives. Some employers use social networking sites on the Internet as yet another bank of information to check out potential new recruits, while others believe such checks invade candidates' privacy.

TIP

BE AWARE OF REPUTATION

Type your organization's name into a search engine to check on-line mentions to know what employees are saying about your own organization.

Knowing what to look for

Research by job site CareerBuilder.com revealed that in the US, one-third of the hiring managers who screened candidates via social networking profiles reported they dismissed some from consideration after finding inappropriate content. Material regarded as deal-breakers included information about using drugs, badmouthing employers or colleagues, lying about qualifications, criminal behavior, and making discriminatory remarks related to race, gender, or religion. However, 24 percent reported finding content that helped solidify their decision to hire a particular candidate, if, for example, their profile reflected achievement or creativity. To use such sites effectively, you must know what information you are looking for.

CASE STUDY

Enterprise Rent-A-Car

There's no doubt that social networking sites are a major phenomenon, but not all of the world's top employers are inclined to use them—even when an employer is well-known as a top employer of graduates, who are generally among the dominant users of such sites. To the accompaniment of considerable news coverage, the European human resources director of international car rental organization Enterprise Rent-A-Car revealed that her recruiters would not research job candidates via social networking sites. According to her, scrutinizing personal web pages invades the candidates' privacy. By using personal web pages for business purposes, employers would be blurring the lines between what is personal and what is business, she told interviewers.

Exploring profiles on-line

To find out more about a candidate's professional affiliations, contacts, and background on-line, first type that person's name into your search engine to see if any web mentions come up. If a listing appears, click on the link related to a business-focused social networking site. Ultimately, however, it may be best simply to avoid social networking sites such as Facebook and MySpace, which focus more on personal life.

Your decision to research candidates on social networking sites must be based on your organization's values. If your organization has a conservative culture, exploring such sites may result in your finding material that turns a previously appealing candidate into a less interesting one. But if your organization has a creative culture, your view of some candidates could be enhanced if their web pages feature an innovative design or information about a meaningful project.

TIP

CHECK YOUR LIABILITY

If you outsource any recruitment to third parties, make sure they follow your policy on using, or not using, social networking sites to check out candidates. Using the sites inappropriately could mean joint liability.

CHECKING SOCIAL NETWORKING SITES

FAST TRACK	OFF TRACK
Visiting professionally-focused sites	Visiting sites that are used primarily for socializing with friends and family
Considering professional references on candidates' profiles	Looking for embarrassing photos or video clips
Looking at the on-line networking groups that they belong to	Seeking out personal details, such as a current pregnancy, which does not affect hiring decisions
Studying their public profiles for work-related information	Making inappropriate contact with candidates

Chapter 4

Making the final decision

The information required to make the hiring decision is in your hands, but the difficult task of analyzing and prioritizing the strengths and potential of each candidate still lies ahead—as does the decision of choosing the best person for the role.

Aligning goals

Hiring a new person into your organization is more than simply filling a slot. It is not enough for the new hire to meet today's needs; in this fast-moving world, new recruits must be capable of growing and developing along with the organization.

TIP

PREDICT THE BEST DEVELOPERS

Remember that past performance is a strong indicator of future performance. Candidates with a track record of embracing development elsewhere are likely to embrace it at a new job.

Developing tomorrow's team

To position themelves for future success, organizations must understand where they are at the moment and what they must do to reach where they want to go. New skills and new kinds of jobs will be essential to the forward-moving organization. The people who are recruited into their midst now must be sufficiently flexible to be effective contributors to the organization of tomorrow. Think about the candidates you are interviewing and choosing between: who wants to be comfortable and do the same task in the same way, and who seeks a challenge and wants to develop?

Matching values

In some cases, you may be recruiting a person specifically to lead the way toward development and growth. Consider your organization's other goals and values: how do you want to move ahead, and are there right and wrong ways to accomplish this? While it is important to allow and encourage creative differences when examining different options offered by candidates, bear in mind that bringing in a person with fundamentally different values could result in a costly mistake that sets your organization back.

TIP

SUPPORT DURING CHANGE
Sometimes a change in values is necessary for an organization. If this is true in yours, you must openly endorse and back the new recruit's moves to make changes happen in spite of organizational inertia.

Defining the right matches

Draw up a document that outlines your organization's strategic goals and defines the behaviors, skills, and abilities that would support them. Take the exercise further by outlining the strategic goals of the team for which you are hiring, and define the attributes, experience, and abilities that would help them achieve these goals. This approach will require you to understand the direction of both the organization and the team; hopefully, the two are complementary. It will usually be easier to define strategic goals for the organization; individual teams may not always outline theirs. Work with them to do so—however, be warned that this requires care and considerable thought. Then when matching up the abilities, attitudes, behaviors, and skills of each of your candidates to the items on the two lists, you will begin to see where alignment and compatibility exist and where they don't.

ASK YOURSELF... WHAT DO WE NEED TOMORROW?

- What does your organization want its unique selling proposition to be in five years' time?
- What new skills will you need to accomplish that?
- How must our organization develop to fulfill long-term goal?
- What are the requirements needed by today's manager to lead the organization to achieve that goal?
- How do the above needs relate to the position you are now filling?

Assessing strengths

It is rare that a candidate offers all the required attitudes, characteristics, skills, and experience to succeed in the role at hand. Taking a methodical approach to weighing up and comparing candidates' strengths is the key to deciding which blend of strengths is best for the job.

Using the framework

At the beginning of the recruitment process, you drew up job and person descriptions to set out the demands of the role and the experience, character, and qualifications required. You may also have created a decision matrix to give these requirements some sort of priority. When you reach the stage of making a final decision, return to these documents and use them as a framework against which to review the information gathered from interviews, tests, assessment center activities, and resumes.

Weighting responses

Ask yourself what percentage of your hiring decision will be based on information gained in the interview itself—100 percent, 50 percent, or less? If the decision will depend primarily, or entirely, upon the interviews, then devise a weighting system for the responses to each question. Let's say that you decide each answer would be worth a maximum of five points. At the same time, each question would have a different value depending upon its importance to the hiring decision. For example, a candidate might earn four points for the quality of her response to a question, which has a weighted value of three points. The total earned value of her response to that question would be 12 points (4 x 3).

Scoring strengths

If you held an assessment center, bring into the hiring equation the information obtained through the psychometric tests, exercises, and other activities. Create a score sheet or assessment sheet for each candidate. List each element or activity that you "tested" or "scored" them on, and note the appropriate score, points, or place on the behavioral spectrum*. Or you could keep it simple, and put checks by the elements where they performed to an acceptable level and double checks for outstanding performance. What kind of picture is emerging of each of the candidates? Is there one candidate who clearly stands out from the rest? Or are there several with a similar collection of strengths? Eliminate the most obviously weak performers among your candidates. Discuss with your colleagues and any external experts the strengths demonstrated by the candidates who remain contenders, and check if they are the most critical strengths needed by the organization.

*Behavioral spectrum—the full range of behaviors a person may exhibit or actions they might take during an assessment center activity.

TIP

CONSIDER ANY ORGANIZATIONAL CHANGES

Take into account any changes that have occurred in your organization since recruitment began. It may be necessary to reconsider candidates' strengths in light of new priorities.

Linking goals

Next, consider the organization and team goals you identified, along with the list of abilities, behaviors, and skills that are required to support them. Compare these with the strengths of each individual candidate as outlined on the score sheet. Ideally, the candidate whose skills, experience, and other characteristics most closely meet the job criteria will also be shown to be a good fit with the organization and team goals. Remember throughout the selection process that you are measuring candidates against the required criteria, and not comparing them to fellow candidates. Being human, it is inevitable that some discussion will result in candidate comparison, but keep in mind that you are looking for the best match to the job and to the organization.

HOW TO...
MAKE YOUR DECISION

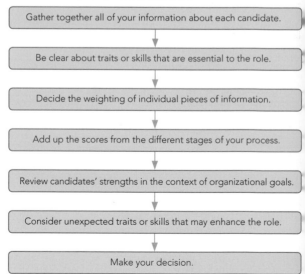

Gather together all of your information about each candidate.

Be clear about traits or skills that are essential to the role.

Decide the weighting of individual pieces of information.

Add up the scores from the different stages of your process.

Review candidates' strengths in the context of organizational goals.

Consider unexpected traits or skills that may enhance the role.

Make your decision.

Experiencing a surprise

As you approach your decision, remember that a methodical approach to hiring is the best way to ensure that the job criteria, person specification, and organization goals are given due consideration when choosing candidates. However, keep your mind open to the unexpected if a candidate has demonstrated an unanticipated skill, personality trait, or other quality that adds a new dimension to their application for the job. Perhaps the candidate lacks a qualification, trait, or experience that you initially considered essential for the role but offers something else that you had not thought about, in spite of your in-depth examination of the job requirements. If you are seriously considering this candidate, weigh up whether you can make that trade-off without it having a negative effect somewhere along the line. But also be clear about which characteristics, skills, or experience you cannot afford to do without. Traits such as integrity and a constructive, positive management style should be non-negotiable, and a specific qualification may be less important to your organization than a candidate's unexpected expertise in a new and exciting technology.

TIP

MAKE THE MOST OF UNEXPECTED SKILLS

When a candidate has an unanticipated skill that could be valuable to the organization, consider whether it is needed now or if a new role should be created to incorporate it.

ASK YOURSELF... WHAT ARE THE CRITICAL UNKNOWNS?

- How well will the candidate work in a team?
- How do they respond to stress?
- What is their management style?
- What motivates them to perform?
- How well will their personality mesh with their potential manager?
- How flexible and adaptable are they to new conditions?
- How well do they think on their feet?
- Are they problem solvers?
- Do they have an unexpected skill or ability that may enhance the role?

Making the offer

The process does not end once you have chosen a recruit. The next stage involves creating a job offer for them and inviting them to build a future in your organization.

Building the package

The salary is one of the offer elements that can make or break the deal. Most employers benchmark salary data to ensure that they pay their employees competitive wages for their marketplace, and offer an attractive selection of benefits. At the least, studying recent salary surveys for jobs in your industry sector will help you to adjust the basic salary that you will offer your new recruits, to reflect the appropriate levels of education and experience, as well as the geographic region.

Informing the selectees

Once you have put together an offer, telephone your chosen candidate to share the good news verbally before you send out the letter. Mention a few of the offer highlights, such as pay and start date. They may ask for a few days to consider the opportunity after studying the written offer, which is perfectly acceptable. However, an attempt to significantly renegotiate the offered salary should be viewed with caution, particularly if a range was originally advertised.

OTHER DETAILS
Confirm a deadline for accepting the offer, a start date, name of the line manager, and the job location.

WORK HOURS
Outline the typical work hours and days, any flexible working hours, and probation period.

REFEREES
Make it clear to the recruits that the offer is contingent upon suitable references.

Making the offer

SALARY AND BONUSES
Be aware of average salary and bonus or commission levels for this role.

COMPANY ASSETS
Advise which assets come with this role, such as cell phone, car, or PDA.

BENEFITS
Spell out in detail the benefits—for example, insurance, discounts, and vacation time.

Obtaining references

Confirming the hiring of your top candidate will depend on obtaining suitable references. You may have explored their professional background and right to work in your country, but taking the additional step of gleaning specific, job-relevant information about your candidate from people who know him or her is crucial to sealing the deal.

EXPAND THE REFERENCE BASE

Consider accepting a reference from a community group or volunteer project who can discuss the person's skills and attributes relevant to the job.

Lining up references

Advise your candidates early on in the recruitment process that if you should decide to hire them, you will need the names and contact details of two or three professional references who would be willing to speak to you about their current or previous jobs. Emphasize to candidates that employment will be contingent on your being able to obtain suitable references.

Requesting information

It is not uncommon for hiring managers today to send out forms requesting information on their new recruits, to make it easier for those giving references to provide information. However, it is best if you can actually speak to a reference. If you are able to speak with someone directly, ask the basics, but also inquire about the quality of the recruit's work, strengths and weaknesses, ability to work with others, and any anecdotes that offer insight into how your potential recruit made a difference in the workplace. Other questions may come to mind, too, but be sure that you ask only work-related questions. Avoid asking anything you wouldn't be willing to ask the candidate directly, such as anything to do with race, religion, ethnicity, marital status, or age.

Raising questions

Hopefully, you will receive information that confirms your best impressions about the person you have selected for the job. However, do make contingency plans in case you get a negative report about your potential recruit. If you receive one less-than-favorable report but others that are positive, ask your candidate for another reference you may contact; there may have been a personality conflict between manager and employee, the manager may have been jealous of the employee, or perhaps that particular job was not a good fit for your potential hire. On the other hand, if none of the references seem willing to confirm information the candidate has given you, you may want to reconsider your decision to hire this person. However, sometimes former managers are simply not sufficiently interested to pass on information, positive or negative, about ex-employees. This should not be held against the candidate; you will have to consider this a "neutral" reference, and ask the candidate for another. Another scenario that has been known to unfold is the use of family or friends as professional references, so be certain to verify the circumstances in which the reference knew the candidate.

TIP

GET IN TOUCH WITH THE REFERENCES

Follow up reference forms and letters with a more direct approach—a phone call—to ensure you get the necessary answers regarding your candidates.

✓ CHECKLIST **CREATING A REFERENCE FORM**

	YES	NO
• Have you confirmed dates of employment and job title(s) during employment?	☐	☐
• Have you confirmed the candidate's final salary?	☐	☐
• Have you asked about any promotions or honors?	☐	☐
• Have you asked about their responsibilities?	☐	☐
• Can they list the training and development undertaken?	☐	☐
• Can they confirm the candidate's reason for leaving?	☐	☐

Sending rejection letters

Probably the most painful part of recruitment is telling those not selected that they did not get the job. Those candidates will no doubt share their experiences—good or bad—with their friends or family, so organizations can only gain by treating unsuccessful candidates well.

TIP

TREAT EACH CANDIDATE EQUALLY

Choose your language carefully so that no one could build a case for being discriminated against.

Handling with care

Failing to get a job you want is one of life's great disappointments. The bottom line is that you as an individual did not offer everything the employer wanted. Being able to empathize with that blow to self-esteem will go a long way toward guiding your treatment of the unselected candidates. Treating them with dignity can create a good impression of your organization as an employer. Even though your attention may be focused on bringing on board your new employee, ensuring that those you did not select walk away with a positive impression is time well spent.

"We received a number of very strong applications."

"I regret to say your application has not been successful."

"If you have any comments on your experience of our recruitment process, we would be delighted to hear them."

Contacting non-selectees

Send all non-selected candidates a formal letter confirming that they did not get the job. The tone must be businesslike, but inject some warmth, with a comment referring back to an interesting bit of information the candidate revealed in the interview, if possible. Depending on the number of candidates you interviewed, you may have time to telephone non-selectees. If so, tell them that they have not been selected, but thank them for applying and wish them well in their job search.

Being positive in your approach

The rejecting letter's main purpose is to tell non-selectees they were not successful this time, but it also gives you a vehicle to encourage promising candidates to apply to your organization again. You could also invite them to apply for specific roles in your organization for which they may be better suited. However, letters to the candidates who would not be a good fit for the organization should be just as professional and courteous as those to the people whom you would like to see apply again in the future.

"Thank you for taking the time to come in."

"My colleagues and I greatly enjoyed meeting you."

"We would be happy to consider your application for the more junior position of..."

Reviewing your process

Once you have nearly completed your recruitment process, go back over the steps to examine the results and see where the process could be improved. Your own notes and the opinions of colleagues and experts involved in the process can help with this.

Looking for "red flags"

Analyze your collated data to look for indicators that your process is inadequate. Warning signs might include too few applications from candidates with the right skill sets, or information gaps about candidates' capabilities. Exchange feedback with the colleagues involved in the process about interviewing style, the relevance of questions asked, and what could be improved.

LOCATION
Make sure you place future advertisements in the places where the most appropriate candidates for the role are most likely to see them.

Measuring return on investment

Keep records of the number of days it has taken to hire for the role, from the beginning of the process to the candidate's formal acceptance. Closely monitor the total cost-to-hire—this will include costs incurred for advertising, recruitment consultants, assessment center tests, background checking carried out by external consultants, venue hire, and staff hours. Effectively managing the time it takes to hire means balancing the quick and efficient filling of the position with not rushing to put the first available candidate in place. Keeping cost-to-hire at a fiscally responsible level is challenging, which means that you must keep tabs on the return-on-investment of each expense.

JOB DESCRIPTION
Ensure that future advertisements explain and "sell" the job, and effectively communicate your organization's brand and identity.

Planning your recruitment advertising

MEDIA
Consider which medium—print or on-line—produced the most candidates, and which specific title or site delivered the best-qualified applicants.

QUALIFICATIONS
Determine whether there was an overabundance or a noticeable lack of certain desired skills/experience offered by candidates.

DIVERSITY
Check whether candidates had similar backgrounds, or they represented the diversity of your customers, clients, and geographic location.

Bringing new staff on board

The candidate has been chosen and has accepted your offer. Now it is time to make sure that the transition from candidate to employee is seamless. Lay the groundwork for a successful future in the organization by providing the right information and equipment—and a warm welcome.

TIP

PERSONALIZE THE EXPERIENCE
Select a colleague to initiate contact with the newcomer and be a "buddy" during the orientation, to answer questions, and keep the newcomer up-to-date with office projects and activities before they arrive.

Creating a link

If your organization does not already have a program in place for preparing recruits for their new workplace, it is time to build one. One way to start making new employees feel as though they are already part of the team is to send them employee information, such as a staff handbook, before their first day. Or you could send them a link and log-in for the organization website's intranet so that they can get a feel for its day-to-day goings on as well as benefits, social events, dress code, and the organizational structure. If your organization has branded materials, such as pens, T-shirts, or caps, give these items as a gift to communicate the message "You are one of us." If the person is relocating from a distance, send information about the local area, such as accommodation, schools, and leisure facilities.

✔ CHECKLIST **BRINGING THE NEWCOMER ON BOARD**

	YES	NO
• Have I sent relevant employee information to the newcomer?	☐	☐
• Have I ensured that the line manager or a colleague is prepared for the newcomer's arrival?	☐	☐
• Have I organized a session to explain the team's current projects and how the new recruit is expected to contribute to them?	☐	☐

Planning Day One

Advise your new employees where they need to report on their first day, with directions on how to get there. If there is an organization-wide first-day orientation, plan for a colleague from their team to meet them afterward. Then let them spend the first day getting to know the workplace, their work equipment, and their colleagues. A nice touch is for the line manager to take the newcomer out for lunch on the first day to spend some time over a meal discussing the job, plans for the first week at work, and the team's current projects. This can get the relationship off on a good footing by demonstrating the line manager's accessibility to team members.

Mapping the future

Most importantly, your new hire needs to understand your organization's mission, values, and strategy moving forward. They need to know where they fit in, and how they are expected to contribute to the organization's day-to-day operations as well as the future. Having their job description at hand to review will reinforce their duties and responsibilities. Mapping out a clear idea of the team's targets over the next few months will provide a view of how all the pieces fit together. A well-thought out and welcoming beginning will help newcomers to start this phase of their careers with confidence. And that is one of the best ways to retain the best and brightest talent.

IN FOCUS...
"ONBOARDING"

Top employers now take seriously the need to make joining an organization as smooth and enjoyable a process as possible for its new employees. There is certainly a business case for it, whether applied to an organization's most junior employee or its most senior. Evidence shows that when done well, "onboarding" promotes productivity, encourages employee retention, and leads to quicker assimilation of recruits. Well-planned programs ensure that all the necessary paperwork is completed early on, that they have the necessary work equipment from the first day, and that they get off to a running start with the new job.

Index

Acknowledgments

Author's acknowledgments
My love and thanks go to my husband Steve for his unwavering support and willingness to supply me with my favorite soft drink during this project. Love also to Alfie, Teddy, Jack, and Sophie for their boundless support and forcing me to take breaks every so often.

Thanks to my great team at *Recruiter* at the time of writing—Colin Cottell, Christopher Goodfellow, Ben Jones, Graham Simons, Vanessa Townsend, Adrian Taylor—for their commitment and passion to always upping the standard.

Additional "thank yous" to Uzair Bawany and other recruitment professionals who offered their support, and who regularly inspire me with their professionalism.

And very importantly, thanks to editors Daniel Mills and Saloni Talwar for their creativity, patience, and collegial support, and to Adèle Hayward for giving me this opportunity to take the plunge and embark on a new adventure.

Publisher's acknowledgments
The publisher would like to thank Margaret Parrish for coordinating Americanization.

Picture credits
The publisher would like to thank the following for their kind permission to reproduce their photographs:

(Key: a-above; b-below/bottom; c-center; l-left; r-right; t-top)

1 Constantine Chagin; 4–5 IMAGEMORE Co., Ltd.; 9 Ravi Tahilramani; 10–11 Getty Images: George Diebold; 17cb Zac Macaulay, 17bc Corbis: Randy Faris; 18 iStockphoto.com; 24 Image Source; 26–27 Marc Dietrichc; 30–31 Ted Horowitz; 35 George Cairns; 42–43 Mads Abildgaard, 43 Vasiliy Yakobchuk; 51 Paul Taylor; 56–57 Thom Lang; 60–61 Coneyl Jay; 64–65 Darren Robb; 66–67 Luis Pedrosa; 47bl, 47br, 47tl Yunus Arakon, 47cl, 47cr, 47tr Sergejs cunkevics

Jacket images: Front: Getty Images: Tipp Howell

All other images © Dorling Kindersley For further information see: www.dkimages.com